AF575907

Making
HEALTHIER
Choices
Sleeping
Better
Marty
Gitlin

PUBLISHERS
2001 SW 31st Avenue
Hallandale, FL 33009
www.mitchelllane.com

First Edition, 2019
Designer: Sharon Beck
Editor: Jim Whiting

Library of Congress Cataloging-in-Publication Data
Names: Gitlin, Marty, author.
Title: Sleeping better / by Marty Gitlin.
Description: Hallandale, FL : Mitchell Lane Publishers, [2019] | Series: Making healthier choices | Audience: Age 8-13. | Includes bibliographical references and index.
Identifiers: LCCN 2018003187 | ISBN 9781680202786 (library bound) | ISBN 9781680202793
Subjects: LCSH: Sleep—Juvenile literature. | Sleep disorders—Juvenile literature.
Classification: LCC RC547 .G58 2018 | DDC 616.8/498—dc23
LC record available at https://lccn.loc.gov/2018003187

eBook ISBN: 978-1-68020-279-3

PHOTO CREDITS: Cover and interior art—JGI/Jamie Grill/Getty Images, Yuri_Arcurs/Getty Images, AlonzoDesign/Getty Images, A-R-T-U-R/Getty Images; cover, p. 1—DragonImages/Getty Images; p. 3—amtitus/Getty Images, Neustockimages/Getty Images; p. 5—Shestock/Getty Images, Peabody Awards/cc-by-sa 2.0; p. 7—ChristopherBernard/Getty Images, Mlenny/Getty Images; p. 9—Choreograph/Getty Images, monkeybusinessimages/Getty Images; p. 10—GlobalStock/Getty Images; p. 11—Media for Medical SARL/Alamy Stock Photo; p. 12—vitapix/Getty Images; pp. 13, 16—LittleBee80/Getty Images; p. 15—BSIP SA/Alamy Stock Photo, KidStock/Getty Images; p. 17—vitranc/Getty Images; p. 18—FlairImages/Getty Images; p. 21—lovro77/Getty Images, Sadeugra/Getty Images; p. 22—wernerimages/Getty Images; pp. 23—Lev Dolgachov/Alamy Stock Photo, Kennan Harvey/Getty Images; p. 24—Oredia/Alamy Stock Photo; p. 25—Zinkevych/Getty Images; p. 27—Artfoliophoto/Getty Images, Purestock/Getty Images; p. 29— marcduf/Getty Images.

CONTENTS

CHAPTER 1

Tossing and Turning

Amy Poehler is a famous actor and comedian. She is also a writer, director, and producer. She is rich and successful. You would think that she has nothing to worry about.

You would be wrong. Poehler worries a lot. While countless millions of people are asleep at night, Poehler is wide awake. She wants to join them in their slumber. Yet she cannot sleep—no matter how hard she tries. Poehler voiced her anger in her 2014 book titled *Yes Please*. She wrote:

> I truly suffer at night. Bedtime is fraught with fear and disappointment. When it is just me alone with my restless body and mind, I feel like the whole world is asleep and gone. It's very lonely. I am tired of being tired and talking about how tired I am. I now read articles about how great sleep is and how important it is and I cry because I want it so bad and I am so mad at how great everyone else seems to be at it.

Insomnia is a serious problem. It can lead to mood swings and affect your overall health.

Poehler might feel that the whole world is happily snoozing while she tosses and turns. But she is not alone. About 60 million Americans struggle to sleep. So do many more millions of people around the world.

Many of them are children. One result is that they are tired during the day. That worsens their school work and their play time.

What is known as "insomnia" is an inability to fall asleep and stay asleep. The issue can

Amy Poehler

Another snooze-stopper is soda. Drinks loaded with caffeine provide too much fuel during the day. That energy can keep children up at night.

be short-term or long-term. It can happen every night or just sometimes. It can keep people up all night or just a couple of hours. It can be caused by physical pain. Or emotional issues. Or mental stress. It can strike kids who resist bedtime or who welcome it. Often there are no obvious reasons for it.

Some sleep problems are more common to adults. Tension often keeps them awake at night. So do negative thoughts about past events. Many of them feel pressure about their jobs and their parenting.

Children can also suffer mentally and emotionally. Stress is a common reason why kids lie awake at night. So are problems at school or strained friendships. Or bullying. Or fights with siblings.

Another snooze-stopper is soda. Drinks loaded with caffeine provide too much fuel during the day. That energy can keep children up at night. Being “hyperactive” can be treated with medications. But those drugs can cause sleepless nights as well.

Kids can suffer from the same medical issues as adults. Some of these are stuffy noses, allergies, and itchy skin. Another is heartburn. That is sometimes caused by snacking too close to bedtime. Some kids even have restless leg syndrome. This refers to uncontrolled movements that prevent sleep.

Other factors include house and room conditions. Noises like family members talking or watching television can keep kids awake. So can too much heat or cold. Mattresses and pillows that are too hard or too soft might make it harder to sleep.

If you're too tired to eat breakfast, chances are you didn't sleep well.

Knowing the importance of slumber can motivate kids. But they first must recognize why they do not sleep well. Among the experts on such problems is Gayle Green, who wrote a book on the subject titled *Insomniac*.

If you are smiling before you get out of bed, you probably had a peaceful sleep.

"Sleep is the fuel of life," Green told National Public Radio. "It's nourishing; it's restorative. And when you are deprived of it, you are really deprived of a basic kind of sustenance."

That means taking every step to ensure a restful night. But it also means being aware that sleeping well is as important to your health as eating well. Knowledge can lead to a cure for insomnia.

CHAPTER 2

All About Sleep

A frustrated father wrote to a parenting website for advice. His 9-year-old son could not fall asleep. And the dad did not know why.

He explained that his son would eat cookies and ice cream after dinner. He put the child to bed around 8:00 p.m. The boy would read for a while before turning out the lights. Then he would lie awake for hours.

The parents who responded had strong reactions. Why was the dad giving his boy cookies and sugary desserts just two hours before bedtime? The sweets were bound to keep the kid awake, they said. They suggested that he serve fruit to his son instead.

The father was not alone in needing advice. Many parents do not understand why their children do not sleep well. But it is not only up to parents. Kids should also be aware of the need to develop habits that promote sleep.

The goal of sleeping is to be at your best when you wake up. Your brain needs rest. Your body needs rest. Waking up refreshed and mentally sharp results in a fruitful day.

Waking up happy in the morning probably means you had a good night's sleep.

Kids who sleep well are more likely to remember what they learned in school. They concentrate better in the classroom and at home. They are better able to solve problems and create new ideas.

The physical benefits of sleeping well are also important. A calm slumber aids in the growth of muscles and bones. It helps the entire body stay healthy and avoid illness. It helps injured muscles and skin problems heal better and faster.

Not sleeping well can result in falling asleep in class.

Kids between the ages of 5 and 12 require 10-11 hours of sleep every night. That allows them to be in peak mental and physical shape the next morning. Full rest leads to better moods during the day. That means better relationships with friends and family.

Those who do not sleep well can be grumpy. They don't give a good effort and performance in games and sports. They have less patience in dealing with others. And they struggle to soak in what parents and teachers tell them.

It helps to understand what happens when people sleep. Sleeping occurs in cycles. Each cycle lasts about 90 minutes and has several phases. The first phase marks the change from being awake to starting to nod off to sleep. Brain waves begin to slow down. This phase lasts for just a few minutes.

The next phase is a period of slight sleep. It lasts for about 20 to 25 minutes. The third phase is much deeper sleep. Brain waves slow down even more. So do heartbeat and breathing. There is almost no muscular activity.

The final phase features an active brain and eyes moving under the eyelids. This Rapid Eye Movement (REM) is the time when dreaming occurs. It ends the cycle and leads to the start of the next one. It's best to have about four to six complete cycles every night.

For those with insomnia, those cycles either never begin or are stop and start.

Kids who do not sleep well should learn why. One reason might be "sleep apnea." That is when the air passages become blocked. It can result in snoring. It can also lead to pauses in breathing and a drop in oxygen levels. The issue causes people to often wake up at night.

Kids between the ages of 5 and 12 require 10-11 hours of sleep every night. That allows them to be in peak mental and physical shape the next morning.

Some kids with sleep apnea have to wear a breathing machine at night. This can hinder being able to sleep comfortably.

Some young people want to make up for a lack of sleep. So they rest when they come home from school. Then they do their homework before bedtime.

In many cases, this is a bad idea. Even short naps during the day can make it harder to sleep at night. Cramming homework makes it harder to unwind in bed. The work might remove peaceful thoughts. And the light from the computer can overly stimulate the brain.

Computers are one of many problems for those yearning to snooze. They can cause sleep onset insomnia. Other bedtime demons include cell phones, tablets, and video games.

Devices such as these can have the same bad effect. Their content might keep children awake. Their light reminds kids of daytime. That delays the release of a hormone called melatonin. Melatonin promotes sleep.

Another poor decision is sleeping in. That does not make up for lost slumber. It confuses the body clock. It makes it harder to fall asleep that night.

Taking your cell phone to bed can be a distraction from going to sleep.

Snacking and watching television in bed can affect your sleep.

It is best to find out what is causing your sleep problems and solve them. A regular schedule is the best way to maintain healthy sleep habits.

Some kids watch television or snack until they feel tired. That can lead to nightly insomnia. And it might result in thoughts of never being able to sleep.

Fear of not falling asleep can make that fear a reality. Lying in bed dreading staying awake does not help anyone nod off. That is why it is best to fix a small problem before it becomes a big one.

Computers are one of many problems for those yearning to snooze. They can cause sleep onset insomnia. Other bedtime demons include cell phones, tablets, and video games.

CHAPTER 3

Fixing the Physical

So you struggle to sleep. Maybe you feel too wide awake. Or your leg refuses to stop moving. Or you have a headache. Or your nasal passages are blocked.

You might have physical issues. Do not be afraid of them. Just learn how to fix them.

But first things first. You need to be tired to fall asleep and stay asleep. Playing video games will not help. Instead, go outside and exercise your body.

Run around for a while. Frolic in the snow or enjoy the sunshine. Play baseball or basketball or tennis or anything else that you enjoy. Walk the dog. Ride your bike. Break a sweat.

Regular exercise aids greatly in the sleep process. Use your natural energy. No need to slurp down sodas. Caffeine will keep you wired and keep you from become tired enough to sleep. You should also embrace eating habits that promote sleep. Dinner should be your last meal of the day. A lot of food before bedtime can result in heartburn. If you crave food, fruit or a similar light snack is best. Warm milk also calms nerves and helps you doze off.

Not feeling well can lead to a restless and sleepless night.

Drinking a glass of warm milk can help you sleep better.

Start a routine before bedtime. Doing the same relaxing activities at night has a calming effect. It provides a sense of comfort. A warm shower sends a message to the body that it is time to prepare for sleep. So do reading and listening to quiet music.

Perhaps your parents have set a strict bedtime for you. Do not fight it. Arguing about staying up results in tension. And that will likely keep you awake at night. It results in less sleep than you need.

Perhaps your parents have set a strict bedtime for you. Do not fight it. Arguing about staying up results in tension.

Before you go to sleep, try some relaxation exercises.

Getting less sleep than you need can have several results:

- crabbiness and fatigue
- poorer relationships with family and friends
- weaker performances in school
- worrying that might keep you up the next night

You do have choices to discuss with your parents. Maybe you would prefer a larger bed so you can stretch out more. Or you want new pajamas. Or bigger pillows.

Perhaps you feel your mattress is too hard. Or too soft. Suggest a trip to the mattress store. Lie down on several mattresses. Pick out the most comfortable one for you.

A good mattress can make a big difference in getting a comfortable sleep.

Making requests such as these can help you sleep better. But your bedtime is nothing to argue about. Even if you win the battle to stay up, you lose.

Now let's say that you have followed all the right advice. You have exercised. You have stayed away from sodas with caffeine. You have eaten properly. You have relaxed before bedtime. You have no big worries. But you still cannot sleep.

It is time to find out why. Are you taking medications that might cause insomnia? Medicines for allergies, colds, and asthma often keep people awake.

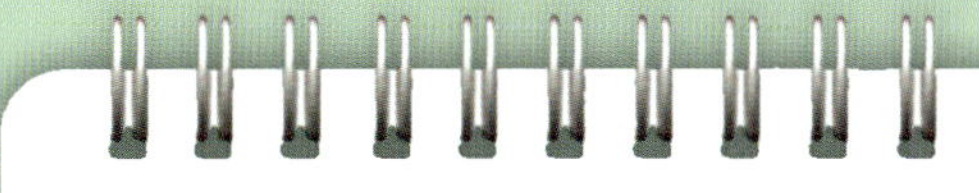

Think about what is stopping you from falling asleep. Or what wakes you up. Any of these issues could be the cause. Do not keep the problem to yourself.

If you aren't taking any of these medicines, you should ask yourself other questions. Do you often suffer from headaches at night? Does your stomach ache? Do you have restless leg syndrome? Are you having trouble breathing through your nose?

Think about what is stopping you from falling asleep. Or what wakes you up. Any of these issues could be the cause. Do not keep the problem to yourself. It will not simply go away.

Tell your parents. Let them know you want to see a doctor. Doctors understand your symptoms. They know how to cure you. But you must follow their directions. Do not take the advice of your doctor one day and not the next. Do it every day.

Many causes of sleepless nights are not physical. You must be aware of mental or emotional issues preventing you from sleeping well. You can take many steps toward a more peaceful mindset. Ridding yourself of worries can ensure a good night's sleep.

CHAPTER 4

Getting Your Mind Right

Your eyes are wide open. You turn your pillow from one side to the other. You scratch your stomach. You roll over. But you cannot fall asleep. Your mind is racing. You are dreading an important test in the morning. You are thinking about an argument with your best friend. You are worried about your brother. He has been in such a bad mood.

It is 1:00 a.m. You have been in bed for four hours. And you have not slept at all. You must get up for school at 7:00. You know you will not get enough sleep on this night. You cannot stop listening to the clock. It feels like it is getting louder. "Tick, tock . . . tick, tock . . . TICK, TOCK."

Mental and emotional issues are a leading cause of insomnia. It is important that you learn how to prevent them from ruining your sleep.

Just two nights of poor sleep can bring about negative emotions. They can result in an inability to enjoy positive feelings. Many children struggle to fall asleep and stay asleep. Anxiety is often to blame. Their biggest fear is often that they will never nod off.

No matter what time you have to get up in the morning, if you didn't sleep well, you'll likely be tired all day.

Some young people even begin fretting hours before bedtime. Or they lie awake at night, fearing that they cannot fall back to sleep. They convince themselves of it—and it becomes a reality.

Do worries about sleep or problems in your life keep you awake? There are many possible solutions.

One solution is to confide in a trusted person, like a parent or school counselor. Their advice could provide the remedy. Just

If you're irritable when you go to bed, this can cause you to have a restless sleep. So you are likely to be just as irritable when it's time to get up.

talking about your situation will give you comfort. That alone might help you sleep. So will relaxing in bed.

Jodi Mindell knows all about it. She works with the Sleep Center at The Children's Hospital of Philadelphia. Mindell tells kids to just close their eyes and rest when they go to bed. She suggests they think about something that brings happiness, such as swimming or walking the dog.

Laurel Crossley-Byers agrees. She runs a life-coaching practice in Canada that helps kids solve their sleep problems. She knows that happy thoughts can produce sleep. It is certainly better than thinking about problems. Or fretting about staying awake.

"When children go to sleep, they know they're supposed to go to sleep, and so then their anxiety level goes up," she told the Today's Parent website. "You're trying to get them to focus on one thought process rather than 20,000 moving through their heads."

Crossley-Byers suggests parent-child talks before bedtime. They should discuss issues that stop kids from sleeping. She urges students to do homework right after dinner rather than just before going to bed. That way they are prepared for the next day so they don't have to worry about it while trying to get to sleep.

So can keeping a daily journal. Crossley-Byers believes that writing down soothing thoughts has a calming

Happy thoughts can produce sleep. It is certainly better than thinking about problems. Or fretting about staying awake.

Keeping a journal can help you release your thoughts.

Getting into a routine that works might rid yourself of worries. It could bring mental and emotional comfort.

effect. Even jotting down a few sentences before bedtime will help you focus on the good things in life.

Getting into a routine that works might rid yourself of worries. It could bring mental and emotional comfort.

And be aware of what you eat, drink, and do before bedtime. These choices will enhance or detract from your ability to snooze through the night.

Sleep experts have many other suggestions. Some might be considered odd. But they often work. Among them is filling a cloth with a lemon balm or lavender flowers. Leaving it beside your bed calms the senses and induces sleep.

A lack of magnesium prevents the brain from relaxing. Eating foods with magnesium—such as almonds, pumpkin seeds, or leafy green vegetables—before bedtime can help. So can wild lettuce or drinking tea with small amounts of valerian root.

Learning about possible cures for insomnia is the first step. Finding the best solution for you can ensure restful slumber. But you must stick with it!

There are several options for tea that can help promote sleep. Just make sure that your tea doesn't contain caffeine! Some types do.

CHAPTER 5

Setting Yourself Up to Sleep

Your bedtime is 9:00 p.m. Your sister stomps into your room at 7:30. She is angry.

"Did you eat the rest of the chocolate pudding?" she asks.

"Yes. It didn't have your name on it," you reply. "It's not like you can write on chocolate pudding."

"That was MY chocolate pudding. I didn't get any. You always steal my food," she says.

Your sister storms out of the room. She is mad. And now you are mad. You try to relax your body and mind. But you are all wound up.

You go to bed at your usual time. But you cannot stop thinking about your sister. You are still awake two hours later. You feel like you will never fall asleep. Your night has been ruined. And you have a big test in school in the morning.

What could you have done differently? You could have apologized to your sister. It does not matter if you were right or wrong to eat the pudding. A simple "sorry" would have made you both feel better.

Being angry with your sibling can result in a bad night's sleep for both of you.

You could have even made more chocolate pudding for her. Then you could have gone to bed with a smile. Calming her would have calmed yourself.

Resolving anger is one step to promoting sleep. But that is not always necessary. What is necessary is a routine. You should take the same steps every night to promote restful slumber.

One important step is turning off all electronic devices two hours before bedtime. Light from a television screen prevents melatonin from going into action. So does the

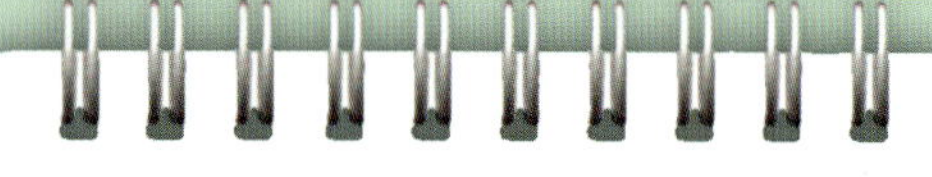

Dreams can be fun to track. Some of them are quite strange. People who find dreams interesting can keep a journal of their dreams.

light of a smartphone or video game. Even a half hour of such activity can keep you awake for hours.

And keep this motto in mind: "Melatonin is good, cortisol is bad." Cortisol is the "stress hormone." Stress produces cortisol. That is why you need to apologize to your sister. Dimming the lights in your room also reduces stress and says no to cortisol.

Another step is setting a regular bedtime. It allows you to calm yourself at the same time every evening. You go to bed relaxed and wake up refreshed.

That means weekends, holidays, and vacations as well. You should make sure you get enough sleep on non-school days. You should maintain consistent bedtime and wakeup times.

The temperature of your bedroom is also important. Many people like their rooms to be warm. But numerous studies have shown that cooler rooms help promote deep sleep.

And if someone says, "Sweet dreams" to you before you go to bed, hope for the best. Everybody dreams. Some remember their dreams more vividly than others.

Everyone has an occasional nightmare that jolts them awake. It is important that bad dreams do not stop you from falling back to sleep. They should also not frighten you when you go to bed the next night.

Most nightmares occur for no apparent reason. But they can also prove the need to reduce stress. Family tensions or problems in school can result in nightmares. So might watching a scary movie just before bedtime.

If you wake up from a bad dream or something spooks you, call out to your parents or go to their room and let them know you're scared.

That is why it is best to resolve problems before bedtime. That is also why you should not be stimulated by TV or computers at night.

You should not fret about a nightmare. But do not keep it to yourself if it is very scary. Talk about it with a parent or another loved one. Think pleasant thoughts after you wake up from a bad dream. You can even write a story about your nightmare with a happy ending.

Dreams can be fun to track. Some of them are quite strange. People who find dreams interesting can keep a journal of their dreams.

It can be fun trying to figure out what your mind and emotions are telling you through your dreams. But they should never prevent you from getting restful sleep.

After all, kids spend more than one-third of their lives sleeping or trying to sleep. That time is critical to health and happiness.

FIND OUT MORE

Books

Huebner, Dawn. *What to Do When You Dread Your Bed: A Kid's Guide to Overcoming Problems with Sleep*. Washington, D.C.: Magination Press, 2008.

Segal, Jason and Kirsten Miller. *Nightmares!* New York: Delacorte Books for Young Readers, 2014.

Strasser, Todd. *Nighttime: Too Scared to Sleep.* New York: Scholastic, 2009.

Websites

How to Sleep Better: 9 Tips for Children
http://raisingchildren.net.au/articles/good_sleep_habits_tips.html

Sleep—Are You Getting Enough?
http://www.cyh.com/HealthTopics/HealthTopicDetailsKids.aspx?p=335&np=152&id=1771

Sleep for Kids
http://www.sleepforkids.org/

What Sleep Is and Why All Kids Need It
http://kidshealth.org/en/kids/not-tired.html

"ZZZ"—The Science of Sleep for Kids
https://www.kidsdiscover.com/teacherresources/zzz-the-science-of-sleep-for-kids/

WORKS CONSULTED

"The ABCs of getting their ZZZs." The Sleep Better Council. http://bettersleep.org/better-sleep/children-and-sleep/

Berchelmann, Kathleen. "Sleep anxiety in children: 10 ways to stop the worrying and get your child to sleep." Children's MD, August 10, 2015. https://childrensmd.org/browse-by-age-group/toddler-pre-school/sleep-anxiety-children-10-ways-stop-worrying-get-child-sleep-2/

"Can't sleep? Neither can 60 million other Americans." National Public Radio, May 20, 2008. https://www.npr.org/templates/story/story.php?storyId=90638364

"Computer insomnia: Why you shouldn't use a computer before bed." Six Steps to Sleep. https://www.sixstepstosleep.com/computer-insomnia-why-not-to-use-a-computer-before-bed/

WORKS CONSULTED

de Graff, Mia. "Why bedtime is so important: Children who stay up too late are 'more likely to suffer depression and anxiety in later life.'" *Daily Mail*, July 22, 2016. http://www.dailymail.co.uk/health/article-3704076/Why-bedtime-important-Children-stay-late-likely-suffer-depression-anxiety-later-life.html

Gongala, Sagari. "Insomnia in children: Causes, treatment, and natural remedies." Mom Junction, November 27, 2017. http://www.momjunction.com/articles/insomnia-in-children-causes-and-symptoms_00118563/#gref

"Helping older kids fall asleep." Berkeley Parents Network, January 2010. https://www.berkeleyparentsnetwork.org/advice/sleep/fallasleep

Iannelli, Vincent. "Childhood insomnia causes and treatment." Very Well, October 10, 2017. https://www.verywell.com/insomnia-and-children-2634255

"Insomnia." Children's Health. https://www.childrens.com/specialties-services/specialty-centers-and-programs/sleep/programs-and-services/sleep-medicine/difficulty-in-falling-asleep-or-staying-asleep

"Insomnia in children." Cleveland Clinic. https://my.clevelandclinic.org/health/articles/pediatric-insomnia

"Nightmares." Kids Health. http://kidshealth.org/en/parents/nightmare.html#

"Nightmares." Sleep for Kids. http://www.sleepforkids.org/html/nightmares.html

Phillips, Kevin. "What is behavioral insomnia in children? Types, prevalence, treatment." Alaska Sleep Clinic, August 20, 2015. http://www.alaskasleep.com/blog/what-is-behavioral-insomnia-in-children

"Sleep and you." Sleep for Kids. http://www.sleepforkids.org/html/you.html

"Sleep tips." Sleep for Kids. http://www.sleepforkids.org/html/tips.html

"10 tips to get your kids to sleep." Healthline, October 25, 2017. https://www.healthline.com/health/tips-get-your-kids-sleep

Vallis, Mary. "Sleep solutions for all ages." *Today's Parent*, December 3, 2015. https://www.todaysparent.com/toddler/sleep-solutions-for-all-ages/

"What causes insomnia?" National Sleep Foundation. https://sleepfoundation.org/insomnia/content/what-causes-insomnia

"Why we sleep." Sleep for Kids. http://www.sleepforkids.org/html/why.html

INDEX